#TAKE THE WHEEL

How to Drive Your Career Growth Within Role and Beyond

Anita Rolls

Contents

CHAPTER 2
WHAT ARE THE FOUR HATS TO
DRIVE YOUR CAREER?

FOREWARD

*T*ake the Wheel: How to Drive Your Career Growth *Within Role and Beyond* is more than a book. It's a guide, a framework, and a mindset shift that meets one of the most pressing challenges in today's world of work: how to empower individuals to take charge of their professional path in a way that benefits not only themselves but also their organisations.

Anita Rolls, the founder of Career Intelligence Academy, has poured decades of experience into this work. Her journey—spanning individual contributor, manager, learning and development professional, and executive coach - has given her a unique perspective on the complexities of career ownership. Like so many of us, Anita encountered the daunting question: *How do I turn the abstract idea of "owning my career" into tangible actions I can take today?*

In answering this question for herself, she created a system that has now evolved into the Career Intelligence® (CI) framework—a transformational methodology that equips individuals and organisations with the mindset, tools, and language to address systemic challenges in career growth and employee development.

What makes *Take the Wheel* special is its authenticity. Anita doesn't just teach Career Intelligence - she lives it. From her early experiments with these concepts while working in learning & development, to scaling them for global use through workshops, self-paced learning, and certification programs, Career Intelligence® has grown organically, shaped by the needs of real people navigating real careers.

This book offers you a roadmap, whether you're an individual seeking greater clarity and control over your work life, a manager striving to support your team effectively, or an organisation aiming to create a high-performance culture where people thrive. It doesn't shy away from the realities of the modern workplace—uncertainty, career plateaus, and even leaving well—but instead equips you with the tools to navigate them with purpose and confidence.

What sets Career Intelligence® apart is its focus on **transformation, not just information.** It's not another "how-to" guide filled with abstract theories or one-size-fits-all solutions. It's a practical system rooted in building trust, fostering meaningful conversations, and generating mutually beneficial outcomes for individuals and organisations alike. I have seen the real and lasting positive impact this can have in wildly different organisation contexts and for people at all stages of working life, from first starting out, to the most senior executive.

This book isn't for those content with the status quo. It's for forward-thinking leaders, teams, and individuals who understand that creating a culture of growth, adaptability, and high performance requires something different. It requires a shared language, a consistent approach, and the courage to transform not just the way we think about careers but the way we work together.

By reading *Take the Wheel*, you're not just learning a methodology; you're stepping into a lifelong practice. Career Intelligence® offers a framework you can revisit and refine throughout your working life, helping you drive your professional path in a direction that's right for you—starting where you are today and evolving as you grow.

As you turn these pages, I encourage you to engage deeply, apply the principles to your own career, and embrace the idea that the journey to mastering your path is ongoing. With Anita's guidance, *Take the Wheel* will inspire you to lead your own growth with intention and create a ripple effect of transformation for those around you.

Let's get started.

Katie Giachardi
Talent & Development Professional

ANITA ROLLS

PREFACE

When I began my career in law in the 1990s, the idea of writing a book like this never crossed my mind. "Owning your career" wasn't taught - I had to learn it. I wanted a fulfilling working life but didn't know where to start.

I faced this challenge repeatedly: as a young professional, a manager supporting my team, and later as an executive coach. The question kept arising: How do I grow without hitting roadblocks or needing to leave my organisation?

Career Intelligence® (CI) was my solution. Initially a personal tool, it helped me grow intentionally and sustainably. As I shared it with others, I saw its positive impact expand.

Today, CI is a comprehensive methodology for career growth and employee development, delivered through workshops, online learning, and certification pathways. Its core purpose remains making career ownership accessible and impactful.

CI uniquely focuses on personal growth, relationships, and outcomes. It simplifies development discussions and strengthens manager-employee relationships, empowering individuals to lead their growth while equipping managers to support them effectively.

This book provides tools and clarity to take control of your professional life. Whether you're seeking personal growth, to empower your team, or to lead organisational development, you'll learn how to:

1. Understand Career Intelligence® and its relevance today.
2. Apply its methods using practical tools and insights.
3. Commit to lifelong learning and growth.

By 2030, I would like to see Career Intelligence® as a trusted framework for career growth across organisations, simplifying conversations and creating mutually beneficial outcomes.

Thank you for picking up this book. I hope it helps you create a meaningful and sustainable working life. Let's take the wheel together!

Anita Rolls
Founder, Career Intelligence Academy

ACKNOWLEDGEMENTS

This book would not have been possible without the incredible support I've received both personally and professionally from so many people over the years.

To my husband Ralph, my Mum, Dad, and sister Asha—for their unwavering belief in me, patience, and constant encouragement as I navigated my professional path. They have been my foundation and support, and I'm endlessly grateful.

To those who played a pivotal role in my journey into coaching and personal development and/or have supported the spread of Career Intelligence® over the last decade: Pippa Edwards, Wendy Johnstone, Erin Kirby, Moira Halliday Alex Dimmer, Alice Todd, Holly Fitzgerald, Jo Herrington, Jane Kennedy, Charlotta Hughes, Katie Giachardi, Antonia Fox, Bukola Bayo-Yusuf, Winnie Annan-Forson, Tim Richardson, Matt Nixon, Neil Evans, Simon Halls, Sharon Prentis, Nidhi Sharma, Nicola Harley, Helen Emmett, Sue Reynolds, Gina Lodge, Benedicte Royer, Heinz Waechli, Michael

Jones, Terri Bailey, Hristina Vaceva, Tanya Tracey, Philip Atkinson, Neil Atkinson, Nicolas Ceasar, Cecile Guinnebault, Emma Pace, John Shurmer, Olivia Jamison, Dori Ben-Chanoch, Sandra Richardson, Josie Gregory, Alan Gilchrist, Duncan Coppock, and Kate Sirrell. I thank each of them for their contributions and support in many different ways.

To all those who have attended Career Intelligence® workshops and programmes - whose stories and experiences have inspired much of what you'll find in these pages. I thank them for trusting me with their journeys and reminding me why this work matters.

To my friends and colleagues who cheered me on, shared thoughtful feedback, or offered quiet encouragement along the way – too many to name here, but you know who you are, and your support made this process feel lighter and more enjoyable.

And finally, to you, the reader - thank you for investing your time in these pages. My hope is that this book empowers you to take ownership of your professional path and create a working life filled with purpose and contribution.

With heartfelt gratitude,
Anita Rolls

January 2025

INTRODUCTION

Imagine this: you're seated at the wheel of your career, staring down an endless highway of possibilities. The scenery shifts constantly: new roles, industries, and challenges emerge, while others fade into the rearview mirror. However, here's the question that matters most: are you the driver, or are you simply along for the ride? For many of us, the idea of carving out a career path that truly fits our aspirations, feels like navigating an unmarked road at night. We stay in our lanes, following conventional routes, unsure of where to start or how to change direction. It's a familiar story. I lived it myself for over 20 years, working across global roles in law, banking, marketing, and executive coaching. Through all that time, one question kept surfacing: how do I take control of my career without jumping ship every few years?

Eventually, I found the answer. Or rather, I built it.

My name is Anita Rolls, and I'm the CEO and Founder of the Career Intelligence Academy. Over the past decade, I've shared this answer with thousands of professionals around the world. My term for it is Career Intelligence®. It's a powerful framework designed to help you take ownership of your career, by aligning your growth with your employer's goals and not by abandoning them. The result? You create a career that's both fulfilling for you and valuable for the organisation you work for. Participants in our workshops often say that this is the framework they wished they had had at the start of their careers.

So, what exactly is Career Intelligence? At its heart, it's a mindset shift. It's about recognising that career growth isn't just about climbing the ladder or chasing external validation. It's about understanding your unique strengths, aligning them with the needs of your organisation, and proactively steering your professional journey, even in a world of uncertainty.

The truth is that the future of work is unpredictable. Industries have evolved, roles have vanished, and new opportunities have emerged faster than ever before. However, while we cannot control the external changes, we can control our response.

Career Intelligence® equips you with the mindset and skills to navigate these shifts with confidence. It's about staying flexible, purposeful, and always in control.

Who is this book for?

While any working individual can benefit, the primary audience is employees seeking to accelerate their growth within their current role and organisation but are unsure where to begin. It is written as a companion book my LinkedIn Course – 'Driving Your Career in a Direction That's Right for You' by Anita Rolls.

In this book, you'll learn how to:

- Evaluate your current career path and identify opportunities for advancement within your organisation.
- Develop the mindset necessary to succeed according to your own definition in a fast-evolving world of work.
- Forge meaningful relationships that align with your career goals and create mutually beneficial outcomes.
- Take proactive steps to shape a career trajectory that aligns with both your personal ambitions and the needs of your organisation.

Whether you're just starting out; feeling stuck mid-career, or preparing for a major transition, this framework is your roadmap to success. It's not about finding the perfect job; it's about creating a career that is uniquely yours and making the contribution to the world that is yours to make.

Consider Career Intelligence your GPS for

professional development. It not only indicates your current location but also guides you toward your desired destination, even when the path ahead seems unclear. And, just like any meaningful journey, the first step is choosing to move forward.

So, are you ready to take the wheel? Let's get started.

CHAPTER 1

WHAT DOES IT MEAN TO DRIVE YOUR CAREER?

1-1: TO DRIVE OR NOT TO DRIVE: THE ALTERNATIVES

Let's begin with a fundamental truth: your mindset plays a pivotal role in shaping your career. It influences how you think, feel, and act—whether it's the major, defining decisions (What's my next step? Which job should I take? Which company is the right fit?) or the smaller, daily choices (Should I speak up in this meeting or stay quiet? Should I work from home or head into the office?). When you shift your mindset, you'll often notice a change in how you perceive your career, even if everything else stays the same.

In this chapter, I'll introduce you to three key career mindsets. As you read, reflect on which one has influenced your past choices, which one defines your current situation, and which might best support your future growth.

The Passenger Mindset

Imagine you're on a bus, but you're not driving. You're simply a passenger, relying on someone else to take you where you need to go. This is the Passenger Mindset when it comes to your career.

With this mindset, you're not actively making decisions. Instead, you're coasting along, letting external circumstances or others' choices dictate your path. You might think, "My manager will steer my career," or "I'll just wait and see what happens."

While this mindset can be useful early in your career—when you're still learning or exploring—it's not a sustainable approach over time. Remaining a passenger means surrendering control, leaving you unprepared for the inevitable surprises and challenges that life throws your way.

The Hitch-Hiker Mindset

Now, picture yourself standing on the side of the road with your thumb out, hoping the next car will stop. You're making choices, but they're reactive, unpredictable, and often driven more by what you don't want than by what you truly desire. This is the Hitch-Hiker Mindset.

With this mindset, your decisions may be influenced by external validation, flattery, or even fear. Perhaps you've taken on roles because they looked impressive on paper or because someone else suggested them. The underlying approach here is to throw everything at the wall and see what sticks.

While this strategy can be helpful if you're unsure of your direction, it's a scattered way to navigate your career. It lacks clear intention and structure, leaving you feeling disconnected and disempowered.

The Driver Mindset

Finally, let's explore what it means to adopt the Driver Mindset. In this mindset, you're in the driver's seat, taking full responsibility for your career journey. You're not waiting for others to take the wheel or relying on random opportunities. Instead, you make intentional decisions based on what truly matters to you.

The Driver Mindset isn't about pushing ahead recklessly. It's about working in partnership with your organisation, aligning your goals with its mission, and proactively pursuing your growth. As the tennis great Arthur Ashe wisely said, "Start where you are. Use what you have. Do what you can." Even when things don't go as planned, Drivers learn from the experience, adapt, and keep moving forward.

This mindset gives you the power to navigate uncertainty with confidence. It's not about being rigid or ignoring the reality around you—it's about taking control in a thoughtful, purposeful way.

Reflect and Act

Pause for a moment and reflect on the key decisions you've made in your career. When have you found yourself in the Passenger role? When did you operate with a Hitch-Hiker Mindset? And when have you fully embraced the Driver mentality? Recognising these patterns is the first step in taking control of your career and guiding it where you want it to go.

So, which mindset are you operating from right now? And perhaps more importantly, which one will you choose as you move forward?

1-2: IT'S NOT EASY TO BE A DRIVER TODAY (EVEN IF YOU WANT TO). HERE'S WHY.

It's often said that the typical employee spends more time planning their annual vacation than their career. Is that backed by statistics? Hard to say. But the knowing glances and nods I receive whenever I bring it up in workshops suggest it's likely true. So why is it so difficult to plan our careers, even when we have the desire to? The reasons can be traced to two main factors—one external, and the other internal. However, there's one effective strategy that can help you tackle both challenges. Let's explore it.

Increasing Complexity in the Outer World

The world of work has evolved into a maze of shifting realities. When I began my career in the 1990s, professional growth followed a clear and predictable path—much like riding an escalator. Do your job well, and you'd steadily climb the ranks.

But over time, I watched that escalator lose its reliability. Organisations flattened out, promotions became less frequent, and career paths grew less defined. Those at the top weren't stepping down as quickly, while others struggled to move up or started seeking entirely new directions.

Today, the idea of an "escalator career" is more misleading than ever. It creates unrealistic expectations of upward mobility in a world filled with opportunities that are scattered, nonlinear, and more difficult to navigate. Ironically, we live in an era of unprecedented career possibilities, yet many people feel more stuck than ever, unsure of where or how to start.

Increased Distraction in Our Inner Worlds

As if external complexities weren't challenging enough, our inner worlds have become increasingly chaotic, making it even harder to manage the first trend. Three key factors contribute to this:

1. **Competing Demands for Attention**: With smartphones, emails, and endless to-do lists,

we're constantly bombarded with distractions. At work, employees are expected to do more in less time, leaving little space for thoughtful, long-term career planning.

2. **Blurring Boundaries Between Work and Life**: The pandemic accelerated this trend, making it difficult to separate work from personal life. When your home becomes your office, juggling multiple roles can be mentally draining.

3. **Mental Health Struggles**: Issues like anxiety, burnout, and stress can undermine your ability to focus on the future when simply managing the present feels overwhelming.

The One Thing That Can Help: A Dynamic Career Plan

So, how do you navigate the twin challenges of complexity and distraction? The answer is simpler than it might seem: create a dynamic plan for your professional life.

A dynamic plan is structured enough to offer clarity and direction, rooted in your values and goals, yet flexible enough to adjust as the world around you changes. It's not about rigidly following a set path; it's about having a compass that keeps you headed in the right direction, even when circumstances shift.

This book will guide you in creating that plan. You'll learn how to cut through the noise, focus on what truly matters, and take intentional steps toward building a career that's both personally fulfilling and valuable to your organisation.

Reflect and Act

Take a moment to reflect: How do these trends manifest in your life? What's holding you back from planning your career right now? Recognising the barriers is the first step in overcoming them. Let's continue this journey together.

1-3: THE FOUR HATS THAT WILL HELP YOU DRIVE YOUR CAREER.

"Where do you see yourself in five years?" That question once shaped career planning, but today, it feels as outdated as a fax machine. Who can predict what will happen five weeks from now, let alone five years? The truth is, steering your career in today's rapidly changing world calls for a different approach—a dynamic plan that adapts and grows with you.

To build this kind of plan, you need a new mindset. Enter the Four Hats Concept, a straightforward yet powerful framework designed to help you navigate your career with flexibility and foresight.

The Business Analogy

Think of it like this: if you owned a business, you'd dedicate time to working *in* the business (serving customers) as well as *on* the business (ensuring it stays competitive and profitable). The same principle applies to your career. You need to work *in* your current role (delivering value) while also working *on* your career (preparing for what's ahead).

Unfortunately, most employees fall into this pattern: they focus solely on their current role until it's time to find a new job. Then, they scramble to network, update their resume, and search for opportunities. Once they land a new position, they slip back into neglecting long-term planning. It's a reactive, stressful, and unsustainable cycle. Just as you wouldn't run a business this way, you shouldn't manage your career like this either.

That's where the Four Hats concept comes in—a proactive, balanced approach to career management that helps you navigate the complexities of modern work.

The Four Hats Explained

Each of the four hats symbolises a crucial area of focus. By consistently wearing these hats, you'll cultivate the discipline to work both *in* and *on* your career, preventing the yo-yo effect and staying ready for whatever challenges arise.

The Chief Operating Officer (COO) Hat

This is the hat you wear to thrive in your current role. It's about operational excellence—delivering results, meeting expectations, and establishing credibility. By focusing on the here and now, you set the foundation for future opportunities.

The Chief Financial Officer (CFO) Hat

Your CFO hat ensures that your career is "profitable" in ways that matter most to you. It's not just about money—it's about aligning your work with your personal definition of success, whether that's financial stability, work-life balance, or personal development. Wearing this hat helps you assess whether your career decisions are genuinely supporting your long-term aspirations.

The Chief Marketing Officer (CMO) Hat

Visibility is crucial in today's workplace. With your CMO hat, you concentrate on building your personal brand, expanding your network, and gaining recognition for your contributions. This hat allows you to attract opportunities, rather than constantly pursuing them.

The Chief Innovation Officer (CIO) Hat

The world of work is changing quickly, and so are you. Your CIO hat keeps you focused on the future, constantly scanning for emerging trends, new skills, and opportunities. It ensures you remain adaptable and relevant, always ready to pivot when needed.

Why Consistency Matters

The key to success is consistently wearing all four hats. Over-focusing on one at the expense of the others can leave you unprepared. For example, if you focus only on the COO hat, you may excel in your current role but risk stagnation if you neglect the future-oriented CIO hat. Similarly, ignoring the CMO hat could mean your efforts go unnoticed, while neglecting the CFO hat might lead you to pursue goals that don't align with your core values.

By balancing these hats, you create a dynamic plan

that's both structured and flexible. This holistic approach empowers you to navigate your career with confidence and clarity.

Reflect and Act

Take a moment to reflect: Which hats do you wear most often? Are there any you've been neglecting? How can you begin incorporating all four into your career strategy?

Keep in mind, the goal isn't to master everything at once. It's about taking thoughtful, intentional steps to align your actions with your aspirations. By wearing all four hats, you'll build a career that's not only successful but also deeply fulfilling. Let's explore how you can start putting this into action in the next chapter.

CHAPTER 2

WHAT ARE THE FOUR HATS TO DRIVE YOUR CAREER?

2-1: HOW YOUR COO HAT CAN DRIVE RESULTS WHICH DELIVER VALUE TO THE BUSINESS

In any business, the Chief Operating Officer (COO) is responsible for ensuring the organisation runs efficiently and delivers value to its customers. But how does this relate to you as an employee? The answer is in your "COO hat." By wearing this hat, you take ownership not just of your own performance but also of the value you bring to the organisation you work for.

Let's explore the two key areas that will enable you to drive results, deliver value, and ensure you have the resources needed to excel in your role.

1. Shift from Job-Based Thinking to Value-Creating Thinking

The first responsibility of your COO hat is ensuring that you're adding value in a way that supports the organisation's success. Too often, employees get caught in a task-focused mindset, concentrating solely on completing assignments and meeting basic expectations. But to truly drive results, you need to think like a value creator. Ask yourself: How does my work contribute to the overall success of the organisation? If you're not sure, take the initiative to find out. Shift your focus from simply doing your job to actively supporting the organisation's objectives. Whether it's improving processes, increasing efficiency, or delivering exceptional service, ensure your actions are aligned with the company's long-term goals.

Reflect and Act

Take a moment to reflect on your current role. How effectively are you adding value to the organisation beyond your job description? Is there a shift you could make to align your efforts more closely with the company's broader goals? Take proactive steps to understand how your work fits into the bigger picture and look for opportunities to increase your impact.

Example

Gary, an operations manager, enjoys the flexibility of working from home. However, his remote setup has led to communication breakdowns with his team, resulting in frustration and inefficiency. In this case, Gary isn't effectively wearing his COO hat. While his work style meets his personal preferences, it's hindering the organisation's success. As a leader, he must recognize that his actions should empower his team to perform at their best, directly contributing to the organisation's overall success.

2. Ensure You Have What You Need to Perform Sustainably

The second responsibility of your COO hat is ensuring you have the resources and support needed to do your job in a sustainable manner. This goes beyond just securing tools or training—it's about learning how to manage your workload effectively and prevent burnout. You might be delivering great results, but if it comes at the expense of your well-being, your performance will inevitably decline over time.

Reflect and Act

Take a moment to assess your workload. Are you managing it in a sustainable way, or are you feeling overburdened in a way that could harm both your performance and well-being? Identify areas where you may need additional support or resources, and take proactive steps to make adjustments. This might involve setting clearer boundaries, seeking help when needed, or prioritising tasks more effectively.

Example

Bina is a high performer, consistently surpassing her targets. However, she's experiencing burnout from long hours and pushing herself to the limit. She mistakenly thinks that achieving results requires working harder all the time, but this unsustainable approach will eventually take its toll. Bina needs to reassess her work habits, establish boundaries, and seek the support she needs to maintain her high performance without jeopardising her health.

The Key: Work Smarter, Not Harder

The key to wearing your COO hat effectively is to focus on working smarter, not harder. Understand what's expected of you and ensure you have the necessary resources to complete your tasks efficiently. By doing this, you'll create value for the organisation without overburdening yourself. Remember, sustainable performance is essential for long-term success—both for you and your employer.

Reflect and Act

Reflect on your work habits. Are you prioritising working smarter or harder? Assess your current approach and make adjustments as needed. Look for opportunities to streamline tasks, delegate when possible, and ensure you're using your time and energy in the most effective way.

Take a few moments to reflect: How effectively are you delivering value in your current role while ensuring you have the resources you need to perform at your best? Are there any areas for improvement? It's time to put on your COO hat and start driving results that benefit both you and the organisation.

2-2: HOW YOUR CFO HAT CAN ACHIEVE OUTCOMES WHICH ARE MEANINGFUL TO YOU

To reach career outcomes that are truly meaningful, it's your Chief Financial Officer (CFO) Hat that will lead the way. In business, the CFO ensures profitability, but for your career, "profitability" goes beyond just earnings. It encompasses everything that contributes to your fulfilment, success, and personal satisfaction. Only you can define what this looks like as your version of success is uniquely your own.

Let's look at how adopting your CFO hat can help you shape career outcomes that align with your values and life goals.

1. Create "Tickables" to Align with Your Career & Life Goals Overall

The primary responsibility of your CFO hat is to define clear career outcomes that align with your larger life objectives. These goals, whether short-term or long-term, should hold personal meaning for you. I call them "tickables"—concrete milestones that you can check off once achieved. These goals will help you stay focused and motivated. Without these "tickables," it's easy to become disconnected or lose your way in your career.

Example

Kimora has been in the same role for several years and has lost her passion for the work. She's not wearing her CFO hat because she hasn't taken the time to reflect on what she truly wants from her career. Without clearly defined goals, she feels stuck and unmotivated. Kimora needs to redefine what success means to her, both in the short and long term. By setting "tickables," she will regain clarity and reignite her motivation.

Reflect and Act

Take a moment to assess your career. How well are you achieving outcomes that truly matter to you right now? Are there areas where something feels lacking? Think about defining your "tickables" to help clarify your next steps and ensure that your work aligns with your life goals. Doing so will provide you with both clarity and motivation to move forward in a way that feels fulfilling.

2. Define "Trackables" to Measure Your Ongoing Success

The second key responsibility of your CFO hat is to define your own measures of success—what I call "trackables." Trackables are ongoing metrics that help you assess whether you're on the right track. Unlike finished goals, they serve as essential indicators of satisfaction, engagement, and progress. They help ensure that you stay aligned with your deeper career aspirations and allow you to adjust your course when necessary.

Example

Chris, a senior lawyer, is seen as successful by his peers. He has a prestigious career and an impressive income, yet he feels something is missing on a personal level. Chris is not wearing his CFO hat well because he hasn't defined his own measures of success. As a result, he feels unfulfilled despite his external accomplishments. By identifying his "trackables," such as work-life balance or meaningful work, Chris can pinpoint what's lacking and take the steps needed to realign his career with his core values.

Reflect and Act

Take a moment to reflect on your own "trackables"—the things that must be in place for you to feel satisfied and fulfilled in your career, according to your own definition of success. Only by understanding yourself and what success truly means to you can you achieve outcomes that are meaningful, both professionally and personally.

3. The Key: Know Yourself to Achieve Meaningful Outcomes

The key to achieving meaningful career outcomes is understanding who you are and what drives you. Only you can define what success means to you, and no one else can make that decision, no matter their intentions. While others may offer guidance, it's your responsibility to establish and communicate your own criteria for success.

2-3: HOW YOUR CMO HAT CAN CULTIVATE YOUR REPUTATION AND RELATIONSHIPS IN A MUTUALLY BENEFICIAL WAY

In business, the Chief Marketing Officer (CMO) is tasked with ensuring the organisation's brand is both recognised and understood by its target audience. Even the most exceptional product can't succeed if no one knows about it. Similarly, as an employee, your CMO mindset is responsible for managing your personal brand—ensuring that both people within your organisation and beyond know who you are, what you stand for, and the value you bring. Cultivating a strong reputation and fostering relationships is essential not only for your career growth but also for creating a professional environment that benefits everyone. Let's explore how embracing your CMO hat can help you achieve this.

1. Manage Your Personal Brand

The first responsibility of your CMO hat is to manage your personal brand. Many employees don't realise they have a personal brand—until they hear the truth in Jeff Bezos' famous words: a brand is simply "what people say about you when you're not in the room." Managing your personal brand is a conscious choice, and it's not about self-promotion or boasting. Instead, it's about showing up authentically and consistently in a way that clearly communicates the value you bring to both the organisation and the people around you.

Example
Angus failed to wear his CMO hat effectively. He was disappointed when he didn't get the team leader role he had hoped for, especially when a less experienced colleague was selected instead. He had assumed that simply excelling in his job would be enough. What he didn't realise was that he also needed to ensure his colleagues and the broader organisation recognized his

skills and contributions. By failing to actively manage his personal brand, he missed an opportunity for both recognition and career advancement.

Reflect and Act

Take a moment to reflect on how you present yourself at work. Are you intentionally managing your personal brand? How do others perceive you when you're not around? Think about whether there's room to adjust how you showcase yourself or communicate your value. To build a strong reputation, it's crucial to consistently demonstrate your skills, contribute positively to conversations, and remain visible to those who matter.

2. CULTIVATE KEY RELATIONSHIPS FOR CAREER SUCCESS

The second responsibility of your CMO hat is to cultivate the key relationships that are vital to achieving sustainable success in your career. These relationships— your career stakeholders—include your peers, direct reports, senior colleagues, internal and external clients, suppliers, and even your professional network outside the organization. However, one crucial relationship that is often overlooked is the one you have with yourself. This relationship, along with those beyond the workplace, is just as important as the ones within the office.

Example

Sabrina, a manager, was taken aback when one of her most experienced team members unexpectedly left the organization. Later, she learned that the team member had felt unsupported and disengaged, which ultimately led to his decision to leave. Sabrina had been so focused on serving her clients that she overlooked the internal relationships within her team. This neglect resulted in a missed chance to boost team morale and retain a valuable employee. By not actively managing these internal relationships, Sabrina lost both a key team member and the opportunity to secure long-term success for her team.

Reflect and Act

Take a moment to reflect on your career stakeholders. Are there any key relationships you're overlooking? This could include relationships with your team, colleagues, or external partners. Are you nurturing these connections enough to foster mutual success? Recognise that building strong, supportive relationships is an ongoing process that requires consistent time and effort. Create a system for staying connected with your stakeholders, ensuring you remain engaged and supportive.

3. THE KEY TO MANAGING REPUTATION AND RELATIONSHIPS

The key to managing your reputation and relationships effectively is consistency. You need to actively monitor and manage your brand and interactions on a continuous basis, rather than leaving them to chance. Building a strong reputation and nurturing relationships are not passive tasks; they demand intentional effort, a strategic approach, and regular reflection to ensure they align with your career goals and values.

Reflect and Act

Think about how others perceive you and how you engage with your key relationships. Are you visible and proactive in managing your personal brand? Are there relationships that need more attention or improvement? Plan to track and nurture your reputation and relationships consistently. By doing so, you will create a positive, mutually beneficial environment where both you and others can thrive.

Wearing your CMO hat means being mindful of how you present yourself and the relationships you cultivate. By managing your personal brand and proactively engaging with your career stakeholders, you ensure that your reputation and relationships work for you—and for those around you.

2-4: HOW YOUR CIO HAT CAN MANAGE YOUR DEVELOPMENT AND PROGRESSION TO HELP YOU REACH MORE OF YOUR UNIQUE POTENTIAL

In business, the Chief Innovation Officer (CIO) is responsible for ensuring the organisation stays adaptable and relevant in an ever-changing world. As an employee, wearing your CIO hat means managing your own growth and staying ahead of the curve—whether that's by evolving within your current role or preparing for the next phase of your career.

Wearing this hat effectively means understanding that development is a continuous process, and progression is about more than just getting promoted. It's about growing in ways that help you reach your unique potential.

1. Manage Your Development: Ask, "How Am I Growing?"

The first responsibility of your CIO hat is managing your own development. It's important to regularly ask yourself, "How am I growing?" Many people make the mistake of thinking development only happens when changing roles or that it's solely about addressing weaknesses instead of building on strengths. However, growth isn't just about filling gaps—it's about consistently challenging yourself to stretch and evolve, regardless of how long you've been in your current position.

Example

Kuldeep has been in her role for 10 years. She's comfortable, well-versed in the job, and knows everything about her work. However she isn't wearing her CIO hat well. Kuldeep believes that growth comes to a halt once you're settled in a role, thinking development is only necessary when a job change is on the horizon. What she hasn't realized is that staying in the same position for an extended period still requires ongoing growth to stay engaged and energized. By avoiding new challenges, she risks stagnation.

Reflect and Act

Take a moment to assess your current role. How are you evolving in your position? Are you being challenged enough to continue developing your skills and knowledge? Even if you feel comfortable in your job, there are always opportunities for growth. Reflect on what new skills, knowledge, or experiences you could be pursuing right now to further your personal and professional development.

2. Take Charge of Your Progression: Ask, "Where Am I Going?"

The second responsibility of your CIO hat is taking control of your career progression. Ask yourself, "Where am I heading?" The important thing to remember is that your career path is in your hands. While the possibilities may seem limitless, this is both an opportunity and a challenge. Though the many potential directions can feel overwhelming, it's essential to be proactive in identifying and creating opportunities for your own growth and advancement.

Example

Paul struggled with seeing any clear progression in his role, so he left his organisation, hoping to find better opportunities elsewhere. However, when he joined his new organisation, he quickly realised it offered similar limitations to his previous role. Paul wasn't wearing his CIO hat effectively. He hadn't realised that career progression doesn't just happen—it's something you need to create for yourself. By not taking charge of his career, Paul had overlooked the possibility of creating his own path forward, whether within his current organisation or by seeking new challenges that could stretch his abilities.

Reflect and Act

Consider where you're heading in your career. How clear are you about the next steps you need to take? Are you actively seeking new opportunities, whether through promotions, lateral moves, or new projects? Take charge of your progression by thinking about where you want to be in the next 2–5 years. Whether you aim to move up, transition sideways, or stay in your current role for now, make sure the path you choose keeps you motivated and aligned with your career goals.

3. The Key to Staying Relevant and Growing in Your Career

The key to growing and staying relevant in your career is being aware of external trends and creating opportunities that align with both your personal goals and the needs of the organisation. This means being proactive in managing your development and taking charge of your progression. Whether you choose to aim for a promotion, explore lateral moves, or remain in your current role while seeking new challenges, there is no one-size-fits-all approach to career growth.

Reflect and Act

Consider your current role and career trajectory. How much are you growing today? Are you actively thinking about where you want to go next? Identify the trends, needs, and opportunities in your field and align them with your personal aspirations. This will help you create a clear, actionable plan for ongoing development and progression that is right for you.

By wearing your CIO hat, you can stay ahead of the game in your career. Managing your development and taking charge of your progression will help you grow in ways that are meaningful to you, ensuring you reach your full potential.

CHAPTER 3

HOW WELL ARE YOU WEARING THE FOUR HATS TODAY?

3-1: TO WHAT EXTENT ARE YOU GETTING THE MOST FROM YOUR CURRENT ROLE WITH YOUR COO HAT?

As you wear your Chief Operating Officer (COO) hat, it's important to measure both your performance and your wellbeing. These two metrics must work in harmony; too much emphasis on one at the expense of the other can limit your effectiveness and potential. In this chapter, we will explore a simple 2x2 matrix that helps you assess how well you're balancing these two elements. The goal is to understand where you are currently operating and take action to ensure you are getting the most from your role—without sacrificing your wellbeing.

The 2x2 Matrix: Balancing Performance and Wellbeing (see Figure 1)

Figure 1: COO Hat Matrix

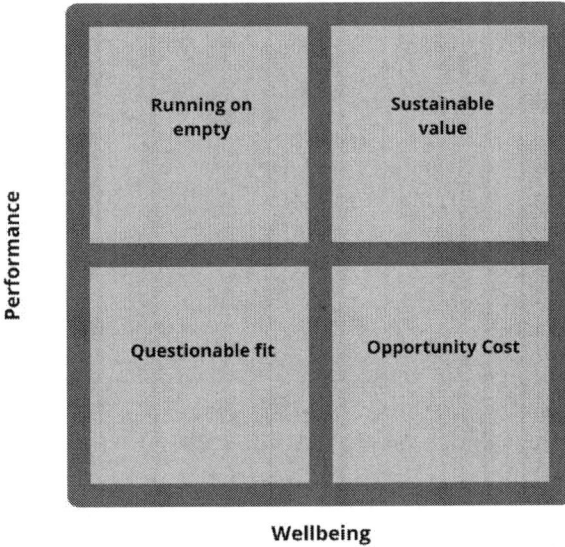

The matrix we'll use has wellbeing on the X-axis and performance on the Y-axis. As we explore each quadrant, it will become clear which one you're currently occupying and what it means for your career and personal health.

1.Upper Left Quadrant: High Performance, Low Wellbeing – "Running on Empty"

If you find yourself in this quadrant, your performance is high, but your wellbeing is suffering. You may be delivering excellent results for your organisation, but you're doing so at the expense of your mental, emotional, or physical health. Perhaps you feel this is just the way things are expected to be, or maybe you know you need a change but aren't sure where to start. The reality is that being in this quadrant is not sustainable. Over time, this approach can lead to stress, exhaustion, and even burnout. While high performance may be recognised in the short term, it's not worth sacrificing your wellbeing for extended periods.

Example

Imagine that Sarah, a project manager, is constantly delivering top-tier results, often staying late or taking work home. She's proud of her accomplishments, but she feels constantly fatigued, stressed, and unmotivated. She's in the "Running on Empty" quadrant. While she's achieving great things for her organisation, her personal health and work-life balance are being neglected.

2. Lower Left Quadrant: Low Performance, Low Wellbeing – "Questionable Fit"

In this quadrant, both performance and wellbeing are low. If you're here, it's important to take a hard look at why this is happening. Perhaps the role you're in isn't the right fit for you, or the organisation's culture doesn't align with your values. It might also be that you're not getting the support, resources, or guidance you need from your manager. This situation is not only detrimental to your wellbeing but also to your professional growth. If you're in this quadrant, it's time to reassess your situation. Be honest with yourself: is it time for a change?

Example
Take James, who has been disengaged at work for several months. He's no longer motivated by his role, and the stress from his personal life has further dampened his enthusiasm. He's stuck in the "Questionable Fit" quadrant. It's clear that his current job isn't working for him, and the first step is understanding why.

3. Lower Right Quadrant: Low Performance, High Wellbeing – "Opportunity Cost"

In the lower right quadrant, your wellbeing is high, but your performance is low. While this may seem like a balanced approach, it represents an opportunity cost. You are protecting your wellbeing by doing only the minimum necessary, but your organisation is not benefiting from your full potential. This quadrant may feel comfortable now, but in the long run, it means you're not growing or contributing to your highest capacity. If you remain here for too long, you risk missing out on career advancements and personal satisfaction.

Example

Consider Mark, who has consciously chosen to limit his output to maintain a healthy work-life balance. While his well-being is thriving, his performance isn't reflecting his full capabilities. Mark is in the "Opportunity Cost" quadrant, and although he's protecting his health, he's not maximising his impact.

4. Upper Right Quadrant: High Performance, High Well Being – "Sustainable Value"

This is the ideal quadrant to be in. Here, you're delivering outstanding results for the organisation while ensuring that you're getting the necessary support, rest, and balance to maintain your wellbeing. This is the "Sustainable Value" quadrant, where both your personal success and professional achievements coexist. By staying in this quadrant, you are setting yourself up for long-term success without sacrificing your health or happiness. It's the optimal place to be for both your career and your life.

Example

Elena is a senior consultant who consistently exceeds her targets while maintaining a healthy lifestyle. She balances her work with regular exercise and family time, ensuring she has the energy and motivation to perform at her best. Elena is in the "Sustainable Value" quadrant, where she's thriving professionally and personally.

Reflect and Act

Now that you have a clearer understanding of the four quadrants, take a moment to reflect on your own situation. How well is your COO hat balancing your performance and wellbeing today? If you find yourself in any quadrant other than "Sustainable Value," consider what changes you need to make to move towards that ideal balance. Whether it's adjusting your workload, seeking additional support, or reevaluating your role, the goal is to ensure that your career is both fulfilling and sustainable in the long term.

Take action today to monitor where you are in this matrix and make adjustments where necessary to ensure you're on the path to achieving both high performance and high wellbeing.

3-2: IN WHAT WAYS DOES YOUR WORK ALIGN WITH YOUR CAREER & LIFE PRIORITIES WITH YOUR CFO HAT

As you wear your Chief Financial Officer (CFO) hat, it's essential to track two key metrics that will ensure your work is aligning with your career aspirations and life priorities: motivation and satisfaction. Both are essential to your overall success and wellbeing, but too much focus on one without the other can create imbalance. In this chapter, we'll introduce a simple 2x2 matrix that will help you assess where you currently stand and how to better align your work with the things that matter most to you in the context of your life.

The 2x2 Matrix: Motivation and Satisfaction (SEE Figure 2)

Figure 2: CFO Hat Matrix

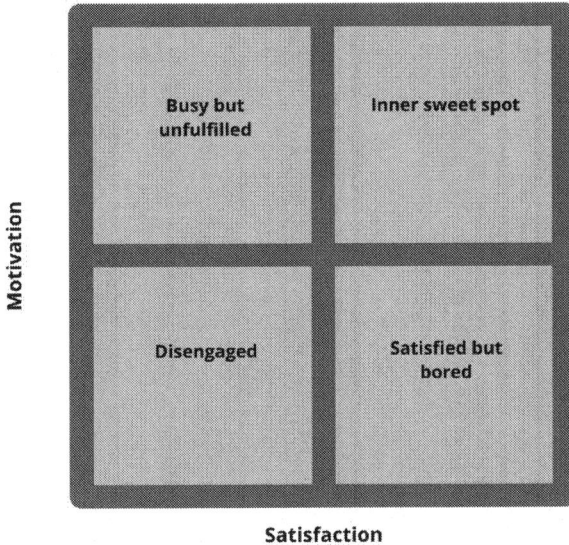

The matrix we're using has Motivation on the Y-axis and Satisfaction on the X-axis. By placing yourself in one of the four quadrants, you can better understand how well your work is aligning with your broader career and life goals.

1. Upper Left Quadrant: High Motivation, Low Satisfaction – "Busy but Unfulfilled"

If you find yourself in this quadrant, your current work may be highly motivating. Perhaps you're working on exciting projects or feel driven by the progress you're making toward your career goals. However, you may also be neglecting other important areas of your life, which is causing a sense of dissatisfaction. You might be trading work success for personal happiness or life balance. While your motivation is high, your satisfaction is low, signalling a disconnect between work and the personal priorities that matter most to you.

Example

Laura is a marketing director who's pushing herself to achieve ambitious targets at work. She's energised by the challenges but is so focused on her career that she's neglecting her health and family life. Laura needs to reassess her work-life balance and find ways to realign her professional drive with the things that truly fulfil her outside of work.

2. Lower Left Quadrant: Low Motivation, Low Satisfaction – "Disengaged"

This quadrant signifies a lack of alignment between your work and your personal aspirations. Even if you're meeting expectations at work, you're no longer feeling inspired or fulfilled. You might feel disconnected from your job, or worse, you may no longer see any meaningful connection between what you're doing and what truly matters to you. This can be a sign of burnout or stagnation, and it's important to act quickly to address the underlying issues.

Example

Derek, an experienced accountant, has been in the same role for years. He no longer feels motivated to perform at his best, and the work that once gave him a sense of purpose now feels dull and tiresome. Derek is not engaged, and he needs to seek out new opportunities or a different approach to reignite his passion for his work and career.

3. Lower Right Quadrant: Low Motivation, High Satisfaction – "Satisfied but Bored"

In this quadrant, you may be satisfied with your work-life balance and the fulfilment it brings, but something is missing: motivation. While you're comfortable, this can slowly turn into boredom. You're no longer challenged, and your career is no longer growing in ways that excite you. This is a common scenario for people who have reached a plateau in their role. While satisfaction is important, without new challenges or goals to strive toward, you risk falling into complacency.

Example

James is a senior project manager who has found a comfortable rhythm in his role. He enjoys a great work-life balance, and his job provides him with what he needs on a personal level. But lately, he's felt uninspired and unsure of what's next. While he's satisfied, he's no longer motivated to push himself. To get back on track, James could set a new personal or professional goal that challenges him and reignites his enthusiasm for growth.

4. Upper Right Quadrant: High Motivation, High Satisfaction – "Inner Sweet Spot"

Congratulations if you're in this quadrant! Here, your work aligns perfectly with your overall career aspirations and life priorities. You're motivated by the work you're doing, and it provides you with the satisfaction you need in all aspects of your life. This is the sweet spot where you feel both energised and fulfilled, achieving a high level of success while staying true to what matters most to you. It's a powerful place to be, where you're not only thriving professionally but personally as well.

Example

Emily is a software engineer who is deeply motivated by the impact her work has on her organisation's success. At the same time, she's able to maintain a healthy work-life balance, spending time with her family and pursuing hobbies outside of work. Emily is in the "Inner Sweet

Spot," where both her career and life priorities are in alignment, leading to a deep sense of purpose and fulfilment.

Reflect and Act

Now that you have a better understanding of the four quadrants, take a few moments to reflect on where you currently stand. How motivated and satisfied are you with your work today? Are you in the "Inner Sweet Spot," or are you in one of the other quadrants? If you're not in the top right quadrant, what are a couple of steps you can take to shift towards better alignment with your career and life priorities? Take the time to assess where you are and develop a strategy to increase motivation and satisfaction in a way that truly reflects what matters most to you. Your CFO hat is key to ensuring that both your career and life are fulfilling and balanced, leading to long-term success and happiness.

3-3: IN WHAT WAYS ARE YOU SHOWING UP WITHOUT SHOWING OFF WITH YOUR CMO HAT?

As you wear your Chief Marketing Officer (CMO) hat, the two key metrics you must focus on to ensure you're both known and known about in your career are personal brand and strength of network. These elements are crucial not just for gaining visibility, but for creating the right kind of reputation that will drive future opportunities. In this chapter, we'll explore a simple 2x2 matrix that will help you assess where your CMO hat is currently operating and what you can do to improve.

The 2x2 Matrix: Personal Brand and Strength of Network **(see Figure 3)**

Figure 3: CMO Hat Matrix

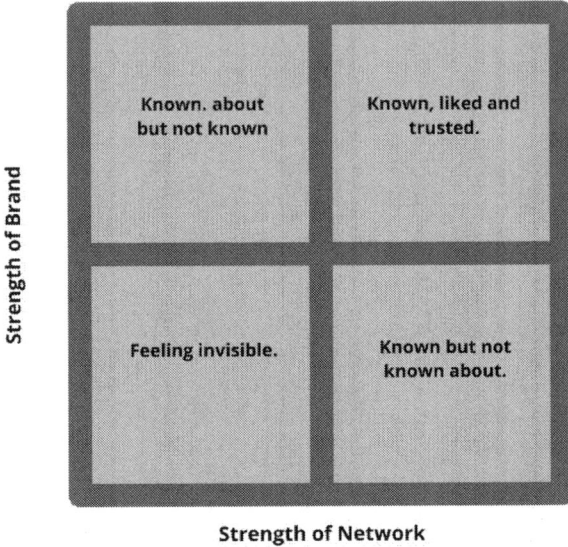

Known. about but not known

Known, liked and trusted.

Feeling invisible.

Known but not known about.

Strength of Brand

Strength of Network

Our matrix uses personal brand on the Y-axis and strength of network on the X-axis. Where you land in one of these four quadrants will reveal how effectively you're building your presence in your professional environment.

1. Upper Left Quadrant: Strong Brand, Weak Network – "Known About but Not Known"

If you find yourself in this quadrant, it means that people recognise you and are aware of your work, but the relationships you've built may be patchy or inconsistent. While you're visible and likely receive recognition for your contributions, the quality of those connections may not be as strong. Perhaps you manage up well with senior leaders but are less connected with your team or peers, or vice versa. This can limit your opportunities, as strong networks are just as important as strong visibility.

Example

Helen, a senior consultant, is known for delivering excellent results and often gets accolades from management. However, she doesn't invest enough in her relationships with peers or direct reports. While she's respected for her work, she doesn't have the influence that comes with deeper, more meaningful connections across the organisation. Helen needs to build her network by spending more time nurturing these relationships, not just focusing on her visibility.

2. Lower Left Quadrant: Weak Brand, Weak Network – "Feeling Invisible"

This is the quadrant of frustration. If you find yourself here, you may feel like you're invisible, working hard but not receiving the recognition you deserve. You might not yet understand the importance of building a personal brand or cultivating a strong network. The result? You feel overlooked, and others seem to advance quicker than you. This is the moment to start acting. Start by reframing how you view these activities. Building your brand isn't about bragging; it's about showing up and letting people know you're there to help. And networking isn't about taking; it's about creating genuine relationships where you can both give and receive support.

Example

Carlos has been working at the same organisation for three years but feels that others, who seem less qualified, are constantly getting the opportunities he deserves. He hasn't put much thought into his personal brand and hasn't invested time in networking. Carlos needs to start by thinking about how to express his value to others and actively seek to build relationships with colleagues across the business.

3. Lower Right Quadrant: Strong Network, Weak Brand – "Known But Not Known About"

If you're here, you're likely recognised for your expertise or work within a specific group, but you may not be well-known beyond that sphere. You might be doing a great job of fostering strong relationships with those around you, but you've neglected the broader visibility that a strong personal brand provides. This could limit you when new opportunities arise, as your reputation may not extend far beyond your immediate circle.

Example

Nina is a software engineer who is well-liked and trusted within her team. However, she hasn't made an effort to build her brand outside the team, and other departments don't know her as well. When a senior position opens up elsewhere in the organisation, Nina is overlooked in favour of candidates who have more recognition across the organisation. Nina needs to extend her visibility, ensuring that her contributions are well known beyond her team.

4. Upper Right Quadrant: Strong Brand, Strong Network – "Known, Liked & Trusted"

Congratulations if you're here! You've mastered the art of showing up authentically and cultivating a reputation that precedes you. You're not just known for your work, but also trusted and liked by colleagues at all levels. This powerful combination of a strong personal brand and a robust network ensures that when opportunities arise, you're top of mind. Being in this quadrant means you have the influence, respect, and relationships to attract new opportunities and pivot as needed in your career. It's the sweet spot of professional success.

Example

Jonathan is a sales manager who is well-regarded across the organisation, not just for his results but for his collaborative spirit. He has cultivated strong relationships with people in all departments, from leadership to his direct reports. As a result, Jonathan is constantly approached for new projects and opportunities. He's known, liked, and trusted, and that's what keeps him in the game for the long run.

Reflect and Act

Now, take a moment to reflect on your own position in this matrix. How well is your CMO hat helping you build your personal brand and cultivate your network? Are you in the "Known, Liked & Trusted" quadrant, or do you need to invest more effort into either building your brand or strengthening your network? If you're not in the top right quadrant, think about two specific actions you can take to move in that direction—whether it's expanding your influence beyond your current circle or ensuring that your achievements are visible to key stakeholders.

Your CMO hat is crucial for ensuring you're both recognised and respected in your career. By showing up authentically and fostering meaningful relationships, you're laying the groundwork for future success. Remember, it's not about showing off—it's about showing up, consistently and authentically, so that others see and value the unique contributions you bring.

3-4: HOW ARE YOU GROWING TODAY AND WHERE ARE YOU GOING NEXT WITH YOUR CIO HAT?

There's a distinct difference between having 10 years of experience in a role and having one year of experience repeated 10 times. The key to bridging that gap is how well you wear your Chief Innovation Officer (CIO) hat. Your potential and your contribution are the two critical metrics your CIO hat needs to track to help you grow and evolve in your career in a way that is uniquely right for you. Unlike the conventional "one-size-fits-all" approach, this journey is personal, adaptable, and, most importantly, aligned with your distinct strengths and aspirations.

In this section we will introduce you to a 2x2 matrix that can help you assess your current growth and identify ways in which you can expand your impact. The two axes—Develop Potential on the Y-axis and Expand Contribution on the X-axis—will guide you in understanding where you currently stand and where you want to go next.

The 2x2 Matrix: Develop Potential vs. Expand Contribution **(see Figure 4)**

Figure 4: CIO Hat Matrix

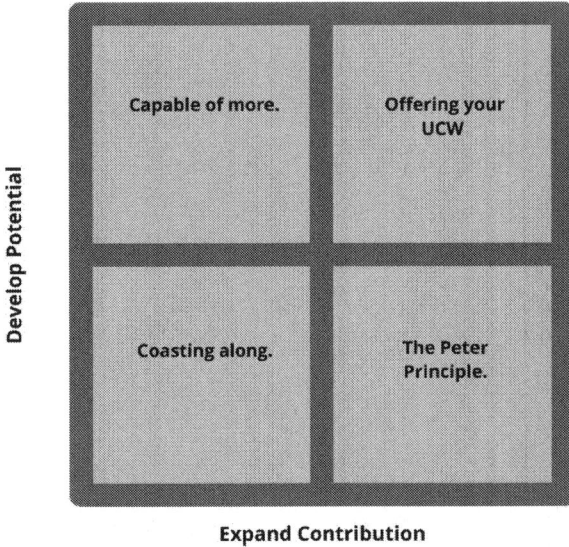

Capable of more.	Offering your UCW
Coasting along.	The Peter Principle.

Develop Potential (y-axis)

Expand Contribution (x-axis)

1. Upper Left Quadrant: High Develop Potential, Low Expand Contribution – "Capable of More"

If you find yourself in the "Capable of More" quadrant, you're focusing on personal growth and skill development, but you're not yet leveraging these newfound capabilities to make a greater impact. You might feel like you're stuck in a role that no longer challenges you, or perhaps you haven't been given the chance to take on more responsibility.

Here, you're developing yourself, but the growth hasn't yet translated into expanded contribution. This could be the perfect time to ask for more responsibilities, consider a lateral move to a new role, or aim for a promotion. Whatever direction you choose, it's important to push yourself further, as your full potential is waiting to be tapped.

Example

Mark has been working in his current role for five years and has developed strong technical skills. However, he hasn't had the chance to take on leadership responsibilities or contribute at a higher level within the organisation. He recognises that he's capable of more, but hasn't yet been proactive in seeking out opportunities to expand his contribution. Mark needs to engage with his manager to explore ways in which he can increase his impact.

2. Lower Left Quadrant: Low Develop Potential, Low Expand Contribution – "Coasting Along"

This quadrant is the most dangerous place to be. If you're here, you're likely coasting, not growing, and not contributing more than what's required. You're essentially stagnating. Perhaps you're comfortable, but comfort is the enemy of growth. Staying stagnant in today's rapidly evolving job market is not an option if you want to remain relevant. Even if you have no immediate desire to change roles, it's crucial to invest in developing new skills to stay ahead. Regularly reassessing your goals and your abilities is essential to keep you moving forward.

Example

Sarah has been in the same role for a long time. She's become complacent, and although her job is stable, she's not pushing herself to develop further. She's not learning new skills or challenging herself. Sarah needs to shake things up—whether by taking on new challenges within her role, exploring opportunities for training, or pursuing a personal development project. Without growth, she risks becoming irrelevant.

3. Lower Right Quadrant: Low Develop Potential, High Expand Contribution – "The Peter Principle"

Named after the Peter Principle, this quadrant reflects a situation where you're expanding your contribution—taking on more responsibilities and doing more work—but you're not keeping up with your personal development. You're pushing the boundaries of your job, but you may have reached a point where you've overstretched yourself. If you're not continuously growing to match the increasing scope of your responsibilities, you might find yourself out of your depth. This is a critical warning zone: to expand your impact, you need to also enhance your skill set. Otherwise, you may soon find that your role outpaces your abilities, and you'll struggle to keep up.

Example

Tom has recently been promoted to a managerial role. While he's taking on additional tasks and increasing his impact within the organisation, he hasn't focused on developing the leadership skills required for this new level of responsibility. His effectiveness is starting to slip because he hasn't evolved with the role. Tom needs to invest time in leadership development programs and seek mentorship to ensure he grows in tandem with his increasing responsibilities.

4. Upper Right Quadrant: High Develop Potential, High Expand Contribution – "Offering Your UCW"

This is the sweet spot—the ideal place to be. When you're in the "Offering Your Unique Contribution to the World" (UCW) quadrant, you're developing yourself in alignment with your highest potential, and you're simultaneously making a massive impact with your work. You're at the cutting edge of your role, and you're able to use your unique strengths to contribute meaningfully to your organisation and beyond. You're operating at your peak, where your skills, values, and impact all converge to create something truly special. This is where fulfilment lies—at the intersection of growth and contribution.

Example

Rebecca is a senior consultant known for her innovative problem-solving abilities. Over the past few years, she's focused on growing her technical expertise and has taken on more strategic leadership responsibilities within her firm. Now, she finds herself not only leading projects but also shaping the direction of her entire department. Rebecca is offering her UCW—making the unique contribution only she can make—and is thriving as a result.

Reflect and Act

Take a couple of minutes now to reflect on where you currently stand in this matrix. Which quadrant do you find yourself in today? If you're not in the top-right quadrant, think about what steps you can take to move towards it. Ask yourself: How can I develop more of my potential? and What can I do to expand my contribution? The key is recognising that your growth isn't a destination—it's a continuous journey. Wear your CIO hat with intention, and you'll continue to evolve into the professional you were always meant to be.

CHAPTER 4

A SYSTEM FOR WEARING THE FOUR HATS

4-1: MAP YOUR GOALS TO THE SUCCESS OF THE ORGANISATION WITH YOUR COO HAT.

Here's a thought to ponder: the most valuable asset you have in your career is not time or money—it's your attention. While you can delegate tasks, borrow money, or even create more time through careful planning, your attention is the one resource you cannot replenish. When it comes to your role as Chief Operating Officer (COO), how you allocate and protect this limited resource can be the difference between simply staying busy and genuinely contributing to the long-term success of your organisation.

In this chapter, we'll explore three essential strategies to help you wear your COO hat effectively, map your goals to the organisation's success, and safeguard your wellbeing by being strategic with your attention.

ONE: Create Priorities

Let's face it—today's work environment is filled with endless tasks and demands. You could work around the clock, and there would still be more to do. I call this "piece-of-string-itis," a state where the work feels like an endless extension of tasks and responsibilities. If you try to do everything, you'll end up burning yourself out. You must be realistic about what you can accomplish and learn to manage expectations, especially your own.

The key to managing the overwhelming load is setting clear priorities. Ask yourself: "What are the key priorities I will get done today, and what are the optional extras if I have time?" Prioritise tasks based on their impact on the organisation and your personal wellbeing. Not every task needs to be a SMART goal— sometimes, it's more practical to define projects that can be completed in stages or "areas" that require ongoing management. Use what makes sense for you in the context of your role.

Consider an example: If your organisation is navigating a significant operational change, your focus should be on overseeing that transition effectively, rather than trying to perfect every routine task. Get clear on what's mission-critical, and leave the smaller items for later if time allows.

TWO: Maintain Boundaries

In a world that demands constant availability, it's easy for your attention to be hijacked by the urgent at the cost of the important. One of the most effective ways to protect your wellbeing while still making a meaningful contribution is to set boundaries—not just with your time, but with your attention. Techniques like time-blocking can help you focus deeply on one task at a time, avoiding the temptation to multitask and spread yourself thin.

But boundaries aren't just about personal discipline; they also involve communicating your limits to others. Set clear expectations with your team and manager about when you are available, and when you need to focus without interruption. It's essential to be transparent about your workload. If the expectations are too high, it's better to communicate this early, asking for the support or resources you need to manage your responsibilities effectively.

Sometimes, you may even have to let things fail to make a point. If you've communicated your capacity clearly and your workload continues to increase, you might need to allow certain tasks to be delayed or reassigned, especially if you're being asked to deliver without the necessary resources.

THREE: Partner with Your Manager

Your relationship with your manager is a crucial component of wearing the COO hat effectively. Take time to understand how you like to be managed and communicate this openly with your manager so they can help you perform at your best. Don't shy away from asking for regular feedback. Use that feedback to continuously improve, ensuring that you're aligned with the organisation's goals while also maintaining a healthy work-life balance.

It's also important to be proactive in seeking clarity about how your role contributes to the success of the organisation. If you don't fully understand how your day-to-day work aligns with the broader mission, ask. This will not only provide you with valuable context, but it will also allow you to make adjustments to your priorities when needed. Don't hesitate to request support, resources, or guidance to ensure that you can execute your responsibilities effectively.

Reflect and Act

Take a moment to reflect on how well you're wearing your COO hat today. Ask yourself: How will I prioritise my tasks today to focus on what truly matters? How can I create boundaries to protect my attention and wellbeing? And how can I ensure I'm collaborating effectively with my manager to align my efforts with the organisation's success?

By consciously mapping your goals to the success of your organisation while protecting your wellbeing, you'll not only be more effective in your role, but you'll also ensure that you can sustain your performance for the long haul. Your attention is your most valuable asset—use it wisely, and it will pay dividends for you and your organisation.

4-2: CRAFT MEANINGFUL CAREER GOALS IN THE CONTEXT OF YOUR LIFE OVERALL WITH YOUR CFO HAT.

The Spice Girls had it right: "Tell me what you want, what you really, really want." When it comes to crafting meaningful career goals, this is the essence of the matter. The challenge, however, lies in knowing exactly what you want—because understanding your true desires is not as simple as it may sound. It's not just about career progression or financial rewards; it's about integrating your work aspirations into your life priorities.

As your Chief Financial Officer hat, it's time to focus on the clarity that will shape your career goals to align with your broader life objectives. It's about ensuring that what you do professionally doesn't just fulfil your job description but also supports the things that matter most to you in life. To get there, let's explore three key actions to help you craft those meaningful goals.

ONE: Write Down Your Success Criteria

The first step in gaining clarity is to define exactly what "success" means to you. Start by asking yourself: What are all the things that need to be present for me to feel satisfied in my work? Break it down into three categories:

Night-time factors: These are the elements that ensure you can sleep soundly at night—things like compensation, job security, a manageable commute, or work-life balance. What must be in place to give you peace of mind at the end of the day?

Morning factors: These are the motivators that make you excited to rise when the alarm goes off—such as the strengths you want to leverage more in your work, or projects that spark your enthusiasm.

Day-time factors: These are things that make your work meaningful beyond your immediate concerns. It could be about contributing to the success of others, supporting your team's development, or creating something that impacts the wider world.

Once you have your list of criteria, ask yourself to rate each one on a scale of 0-10. Where does your current role measure up on these factors? What's missing, and what's already present? This exercise will provide a clearer picture of what is truly important to you, and where your current role aligns or diverges from your goals.

TWO: Think About What You Want to Be, Do, & Have

Set a timer for three minutes. In this brief burst of free thinking, write down everything you desire in your career and life. Dream big, without worrying about whether it's realistic. Let your imagination run wild—this is your wish list, not a to-do list. Think about where you are now and where you'd like to be in the future.

After you finish writing, go back and put a star next to the things that you feel truly passionate about—things you would really like to achieve.

Do this exercise two more times to uncover deeper layers of your aspirations. By the end, you should have a refined list of both short-term and long-term goals. Read it aloud and, most importantly, cross out anything that no longer resonates with you. This will help you focus on what truly matters.

THREE: Partner with Your Manager

Once you have clarity about what you want in your career and life, it's time to bring your manager into the conversation. Share these two lists with them, so they can understand your aspirations and what you value. This is about forging a partnership with your manager to identify ways your current role can be adjusted to better align with these priorities.

Together, brainstorm ideas on how you can incorporate more of your success criteria into your daily work—without compromising performance or productivity. You might be surprised at what's possible.

By communicating your needs and dreams clearly, you may find that small tweaks to your responsibilities or focus can make a big difference in your overall satisfaction.

Reflect and Act

Now, take a moment to reflect on the following questions: What are some practical adjustments you could make to your current role to incorporate more of what you've defined as important to you? And how can you present these ideas to your manager in a way that benefits both you and the organisation?

These are the crucial steps to ensure that your career goals are meaningful, fulfilling, and well-aligned with the rest of your life. By taking charge of your career with clarity and intention, you'll create a path that's truly your own.

4-3: MONITOR THE ONGOING HEALTH OF YOUR BRAND AND NETWORK WITH YOUR CMO HAT.

If your Chief Marketing Officer hat had a motto, it would echo the wisdom of an African proverb: "If you want to go fast, go alone—if you want to go far, go with others." This speaks to a fundamental truth of career success.

Your journey is not a zero-sum game, where rewards are limited, and others are competitors. Rather, your career success is an infinite game, as Simon Sinek aptly describes it: "The players come and go; the rules are changeable and there's no definitive end."

This infinite game requires you to cultivate relationships, manage your personal brand, and strategically grow your network. In this chapter, we'll explore three key techniques to help you maintain the ongoing health of both your brand and your network, ensuring sustainable career success.

ONE: Get Feedback on Your Current Brand

Your brand is how others perceive you—it's what they think of when your name comes up. But perception is often difficult to measure without feedback. So, the first step is simply asking others how they see you. A powerful and straightforward method is to ask people you interact with regularly to share three words they believe best describe you. Reach out to colleagues, peers, direct reports, and even clients, and compile their responses into a spreadsheet.

Once you have your data, analyse it. What words appear most frequently? Are there any surprises? How consistent are the responses? Compare these findings to how you wish to be perceived.

This exercise can reveal gaps between your self-perception and how others see you. It also gives you the clarity needed to make intentional shifts in your brand. If the words you hope to hear aren't surfacing, consider actions you can take to align your presence more closely with the brand you wish to project.

TWO: Make a Career Stakeholder Map

As the saying goes, you can't manage what you can't see. The same holds true for relationships. To monitor the health of your professional network, you need to visualise it. This is where a career stakeholder map comes into play. List all the key relationships that impact your work and career—both inside and outside your organisation. Include your peers, direct reports, senior colleagues, and internal clients, but don't stop there. Extend the map to include external relationships with clients, suppliers, and even regulators. Don't forget to account for the relationships closest to home, including those with family and friends, as they also play a role in your work-life balance.

Once you have your list, assess the "health" of each relationship using a simple Red, Amber, Green (RAG) system.

Are any relationships underperforming? Red or amber relationships require attention, and this map will help you prioritise where to invest your time and energy.

THREE: Partner with Your Manager

To keep your brand and network aligned with your goals, it's essential to engage with your manager in an open and constructive way.

Share the results of your brand feedback and your career stakeholder map with them. Invite their feedback on how they perceive you and ask for suggestions on how you can show up more effectively

This conversation doesn't just help you gain clarity on your brand; it's also an opportunity to increase your visibility. Discuss how you can improve not only your own visibility but also that of your team.

By helping raise your team's profile within the organisation and beyond, you can create a ripple effect that strengthens your professional network while driving career success for everyone involved.

Reflect and Act

Now, take a moment to reflect: How would you like others to perceive you? What actions can you take to influence this perception positively? And, looking at your career stakeholder map, what steps will you take to improve relationships that are less than optimal? By continuously monitoring and managing your brand and network, you'll ensure that you're not just playing the infinite game—you're thriving in it.

4-4: STAY RELEVANT AND MOVE FORWARDS IN A WAY THAT'S RIGHT FOR YOU WITH YOUR CIO HAT.

The late Theodore Levitt, a Harvard Business School professor, famously said, "If creativity is thinking up new things, innovation is doing new things." This advice is central to the role of your Chief Innovation Officer (CIO) hat. As you navigate the rapidly changing landscape of work and life, it's not enough to just come up with fresh ideas—you must take action to drive innovation and keep evolving. In this chapter, we'll explore three practical ways your CIO hat can help you stay relevant, adapt, and move forward in a way that suits you and your unique path.

ONE: Treat Yourself as a "Work in Progress"

In the past, seeing yourself as a "work in progress" may have carried negative connotations—suggesting you weren't good enough yet or that you weren't ready for the next step. Today, however, this mindset is essential.

Whether we describe the world as VUCA (Volatile, Uncertain, Complex, and Ambiguous) or BANI (Brittle, Anxious, Non-Linear, and Incomprehensible), the truth is clear: the world of work is constantly evolving, and the pace of change is only increasing.

If you don't view yourself as a work in progress, you risk stagnating. To remain relevant, you must be committed to continuous self-improvement. Treat yourself as a living, breathing project. Recognise the areas in which you need to improve, and take action to address weaknesses while also honing your strengths. Focus on not just what you can do, but on who you are becoming in the process. Embrace every setback, failure, or challenge as an opportunity to learn and grow. This mindset will help you stay nimble and ready to adapt to new opportunities, ensuring you never become complacent.

TWO: Notice Opportunities to Progress That May Not Be Immediately Obvious

It's easy to feel stuck in your current role, especially when there aren't any obvious open positions in the organisation. However, if you're waiting for a job title to change or a position to open up on the organisational chart, you might be missing out. Innovation isn't just about inventing new products or services—it's also about spotting opportunities where others see none. You have the power to create your own opportunities. Don't wait for the organisation to tell you where your next role is; instead, identify opportunities that align with your skills and passions, and pitch them internally. Look for ways you can bring new value to your team, department, or organisation. As Levitt said, "Innovation is seeing what everybody has seen and thinking what nobody has thought." Don't be afraid to think outside the box and propose new roles or projects that could drive the business forward. The ability to recognise and seize such opportunities will keep you relevant and position you as an innovator within your organisation.

THREE: Partner with Your Manager

To truly innovate and move forward, you need to have a strong partnership with your manager. Share your observations about the opportunities you see and the roles you believe could benefit both you and the business. Ask for feedback on your ideas and get your manager's perspective on where the organisation is heading strategically. Understanding your organisation's direction will help you align your personal goals with the broader objectives of the business. Don't hesitate to approach your manager with your own ideas for career progression. Be open to their suggestions and guidance on how you can align your growth with the organisation's evolving needs. This collaboration will not only help you progress but also strengthen your relationship with your manager, fostering a sense of trust and mutual support.

Reflect and Act

Take a few moments to consider how you are growing today. What steps can you take to evolve further? Are there opportunities within your organisation that you could leverage to add more value? By viewing yourself as a work in progress, identifying opportunities that align with your strengths, and working closely with your manager, you'll stay relevant and continuously move forward in your career, innovating as you go.

ANITA ROLLS

CONCLUSION

Today there is a profound opportunity to make a meaningful contribution through your work in a way that's right for you. The world is changing rapidly, and so are the ways we define success and fulfilment in our professional lives. With this opportunity comes the responsibility to take control of your growth and shape your future.

The key message of this book is simple yet powerful: You can drive your career in the direction that's right for you, regardless of external circumstances. Much like learning to drive a car, driving your career requires consistent effort, attention, and practice. This means managing your four hats—the Chief Innovation Officer (CIO) hat, Chief Operating Officer (COO) hat, Chief Financial Officer (CFO) hat, and Chief Marketing Officer (CMO) hat - on an ongoing basis to ensure continuous growth aligned with your values, strengths, and goals.

Each hat plays a vital role in your professional

growth. Your CFO hat helps you set meaningful career goals based on your values and aspirations. Your COO hat ensures your current work is effective and sustainable by focusing on priorities, boundaries, and partnerships. Your CMO hat ensures you actively manage your personal brand and relationships, building a network that supports both career and personal well-being. And your CIO hat helps you stay innovative and adaptable by treating yourself as a work in progress, spotting growth opportunities, and learning continuously.

By practising the management of these four hats, you can contribute at your highest level, unlock your potential, and future-proof your career. You'll adapt to organisational and industry changes while staying relevant. More importantly, you'll be in a stronger position to have impactful conversations with your manager, aligning your goals with organisational success.

This is a pivotal moment. The more individuals who take ownership of their growth, the more we can collectively address the challenges of today's world. Your professional path is not fixed—it's an evolving journey. The tools and techniques you've learned here empower you to take the wheel and move forward with clarity and purpose.

Wishing you every success on this journey. The road ahead may be uncertain, but with the right mindset, skills, and tools, you are more than capable of navigating it. The world is waiting for your contribution—so go ahead, take the wheel.

WHERE NEXT?

If you have found the content in this book useful, you may want to consider taking the next step and getting your Career Intelligence® Driver Certificate. This will take the principles you've read here to the next level as you learn to apply them to create lasting transformation in how you manage your career.

You can earn your Career Intelligence® Certificate by attending our Live Webinar Series, the link is https://lnkd.in/e8wEBgFY.

You can also take the training in your organisation if it offers Career Intelligence® or via a Certified Career Intelligence® Practitioner.

More details of all our offerings and resources to help you take the wheel are available on our website
www.career.intelligenceacademy.com

Printed in Great Britain
by Amazon